STILL SMALL VOICE

ALLEN
BROKKEN

Unit Study

CONTENTS

1. Introduction
2. Teacher Guide
3. Week One: A SMALL VOICE
   a. Day One (Chapters One & Two)
   b. Day Two (Chapters Three & Four)
   c. Day Three (Chapters Five & Six)
   d. Day Four (Chapters Seven & Eight)
   e. Day Five (Chapters Nine)
4. Week Two: THE LOST
   a. Day One (Chapters Ten & Eleven)
   b. Day Two (Chapters Twelve & Thirteen)
   c. Day Three (Chapters Fourteen & Fifteen)
   d. Day Four (Chapters Sixteen & Seventeen)
   e. Day Five (Chapters Eighteen)
5. Week Three: IN THE BELLY
   a. Day One (Chapters Nineteen & Twenty)
   b. Day Two (Chapters Twenty-one & Twenty-two)
   c. Day Three (Chapters Twenty-three & Twenty-four)
   d. Day Four (Chapters Twenty-five & Twenty-six)
   e. Day Five (Chapters Twenty-seven)
6. Week Four: HOLY SPIRIT
   a. Day One (Chapters Twenty-eight & Twenty-nine)
   b. Day Two (Chapters Thirty & Thirty-one)
   c. Day Three (Chapters Thirty-two & Thirty-three)
   d. Day Four (Chapters Thirty-four & Thirty-five)
   e. Day Five (Chapters Thirty-six)
7. Answer Key
8. Towers of Light Series

ALLEN BROKKEN

Allen Brokken is a teacher at heart, a husband and father most of all. He's a joyful writer by the abundant grace of God. He began writing the Towers of Light series for his own children to help him illustrate the deep truths of the Bible in an engaging and age-appropriate way. He's dedicated fifteen years of his life to volunteer roles in children's ministry and youth development.

Now that his own children are off to college, he's sharing his life experiences on social media @allenbrokkenauthor and through his blog https://allenbrokkenauthor.com/blog.

INTRODUCTION

Dear Reader,

When my children were middle-grade readers, I had a tough time finding adventure stories they could enjoy that also emphasized Biblical truths. So I began telling them a story about life on the frontier, weaving in points of the faith that I felt they should learn. As the story developed, a unique world of pets with fantastic powers and holy weapons emerged to help the young characters hold back the forces of darkness.

The *Still Small Voice: A Unit Study for Homeschoolers* is a supplement to those tales of adventure. It digs deeper into the spiritual aspects of the story from a Christian perspective. Over the next four weeks, your students will study passages from the story to highlight lessons from scripture and their real life application. There are also activity pages and memory verses to help them internalize the key messages in *Still Small Voice*.

I hope you enjoy the story as much as my own children did.

May God bless you richly,

Allen Brokken

STILL SMALL VOICE

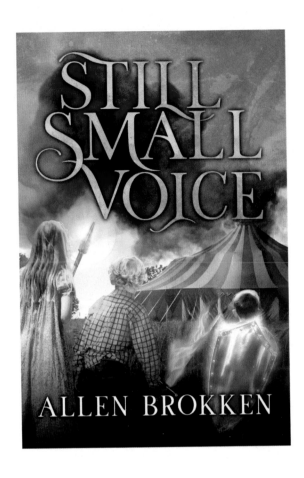

Because of their faith, twelve-year-old Lauren and her younger brothers, Aiden and Ethan, prevailed in the battle for the Tower of Light. But their victory did not stop the Dark One. Darkness continues to spread across Zoura's frontier.

Now, in a vision, Mother tells them to light a second tower in Blooming Glen. Before they can set out on their journey with the Knight Protector, their Uncle arrives with a different set of instructions. He doesn't trust the Knight Protector or the Mighty Mercenaries and believes the children should go to their grandparent's house.

Unyielding in his belief, Uncle unknowingly leads the children off their path. And a misguided acolyte follows them. Lurking in the shadows, he strikes at every opportunity as the dark forces prepare to descend.

Lauren, Aiden, and Ethan are Zoura's last defense. Can they convince their Uncle of the truth—that he must listen to the still small voice—and make it to Blooming Glen before the Dark One's forces overtake them?

Fans of *Little House on the Prairie* will feel at home in the series' classic farmstead setting, and the sincerity of the children's love for one another—nurtured by the example of their parents—will bring a smile to readers and listeners of all ages.

TEACHER GUIDE

EDUCATIONAL GOALS

The *Still Small Voice Unit Study* was developed for the second book in the Towers of Light series, a Christian fantasy adventure for middle-grade readers. It combines Biblical values and educational activities in four weeks of supplemental curriculum.

Story passages, chapter assignments, activities, and thoughtful questions foster Biblical discussion while exercising reading comprehension and critical thinking skills. Vocabulary exercises and puzzles expand students' vocabulary and provide an opportunity for students to use their references skills while also exercising their critical thinking skills. Memory verse copy work helps students learn scripture as they practice their handwriting, and coloring sheets offer a fun opportunity for creative expression.

SUGGESTED PACING

This unit study is designed to be completed within four weeks. Each week includes around sixty pages of story content, which can be read aloud or independently. Students are encouraged to keep a reading journal for their memory verse copy work, vocabulary exercises, and to record their answers to the reading questions.

DAYS ONE THROUGH FOUR

- In their reading journal, have students copy the MEMORY VERSE and complete the VOCABULARY EXERCISE.
- Complete the DAILY READING assignment, aloud or independently.
- Read the STORY PASSAGE aloud and discuss the connection question as a group.
- Have students record their answers to the PASSAGE QUESTIONS in their journal. Answers may also be discussed as a group.

DAY FIVE

- Complete the DAILY READING assignment, aloud or independently.
- Have students recite the MEMORY VERSE.
- Use the COLORING PAGE, PUZZLE, and ACTIVITY as a fun way to wrap up the week.

TOWERS OF LIGHT

WEEK ONE
A SMALL VOICE

Memory Verse:
"And after the earthquake a fire; but the LORD was not in the fire: and after the fire a still small voice."
—1 Kings 19:12 KJV

AIDEN

VOCABULARY

WORD LIST

As part of your daily work this week, you'll need to use a dictionary and a thesaurus to look up definitions, synonyms, and antonyms for the words below.

CRESCENDO   METAPHOR   PROLOGUE
LACQUER   PANTOMIME   SILHOUETTE

SECRET MESSAGE

This week's vocabulary words have been used to form the message below, but it's been encrypted to keep it a secret. Determine which letter in the alphabet corresponds to each number to decode the message.

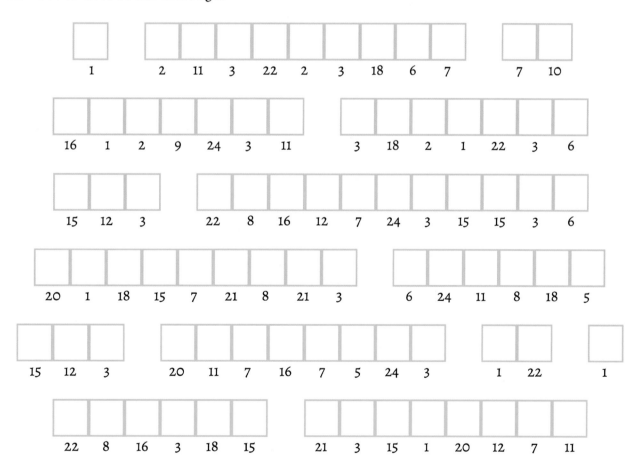

DAY ONE

MEMORY VERSE, VOCABULARY & READING

In your reading journal, copy this week's memory verse and vocabulary definitions. Then, read chapters one and two in the book.

STORY PASSAGE

Knight Protector continued, "This is all so very complicated. But it is clear you are all clever and keep your own counsel on what is best." The warrior rubbed the top of his head.

Ethan winced. *We really conked him in his wonkus last night.*

"You will not just obey me because I am your elder." The old knight looked to each of the children staring into their eyes. "With the deception of the bishop and even my own behavior, it has to be difficult for you to trust anyone. Oh… where to begin." Knight Protector sighed.

"Pray!" Ethan blurted out. He had a plate of bacon and flapjacks in front of him, and his stomach was aching.

"What?" Knight Protector sat back in his chair, wide-eyed at this.

"You said you didn't know where to begin. Daddy always says when you don't know what to do, pray." Ethan folded his hands together. "Plus, we can't eat if we don't pray, and I'm starving."

"You are right, of course. This is your home and your table. Would you want to ask for the Lord's blessing for us?" Knight Protector asked.

HAVE YOU EVER PRAYED FOR GUIDENCE?

PASSAGE QUESTIONS

Read the STORY PASSAGE and answer the following questions in your reading journal.

1. What does the Knight Protector mean when he says "keep your own counsel"?
2. Which sentence supports the previous answer?
3. When Ethan tells the Knight Protector to pray, what do you think he is most concerned about?
4. Which sentence supports the previous answer?

> ### Joke of the Day
>
> Have you heard Optimus Prime is writing a book?
> It's an AUTOBOT-ography.

DAY TWO

MEMORY VERSE, VOCABULARY & READING

In your reading journal, copy this week's memory verse and list three synonyms for each vocabulary word. Then, read chapters three and four in the book.

STORY PASSAGE

Aiden wasn't buying it. *I don't think the Lord would let bad stuff go on if a warrior like the Knight Protector could do something about it.* Aiden balled his fists and put them on his hips. "But, if the small voice told you to find the Darkness machine, why didn't you knock it down before we got there?"

Knight Protector leaned forward in his chair with his hands on the arms and looked straight at Aiden. "It was the Spirit's promptings that helped me to find the Darkness generator. Then, the still small voice told me to wait and see. And low and behold, I saw a young boy wield the sword of Gabriel and smite the Darkness. That was a most glorious sight indeed."

"The sword of Gabriel? You mean the archangel Gabriel from the good book?" Lauren blurted out unexpectedly. This caused Aiden to take a step back.

"Well, maybe not 'the' sword of Gabriel. It stands watch over the garden. But a fiery sword of the type only wielded by the angels." Knight Protector patted the Good Book to emphasize his point.

Aiden's mind swirled at the thought that his sword may have been wielded by angels.

HOW DO YOU KNOW WHEN THE HOLY SPIRIT IS GUIDING YOU?

PASSAGE QUESTIONS

Read the STORY PASSAGE and answer the following questions in your reading journal.

1. What did the Knight Protector discover?
2. How did Aiden feel about the Knight Protector's choice of action regarding the discovery?
3. Which sentence supports the previous answer?
4. Why did the Knight Protector choose the action he took?

> **Joke of the Day**
>
> Want to hear a joke about a piece of paper?
>
> Nevermind. It's tear-able.

DAY THREE

MEMORY VERSE, VOCABULARY & READING

In your reading journal, copy this week's memory verse and list three antonyms for each vocabulary word. Then, read chapters five and six in the book.

STORY PASSAGE

Ethan broke in before Lauren could respond, "He was going back to town to make plans to take us to Blooming Glen, where there are a lot of knight protectors, and the light is safe. Just like my dream."

Oh no! Ethan, why couldn't you keep quiet? Lauren just knew they were sunk now.

"Well, I don't know about all this other stuff yer saying." Uncle reached into his cloak and pulled out a scroll with a seal on it. "But yer pa said that if anything ever happened to him and yer ma, you should come live with Gran in Fairfields."

We just had this conversation. Lauren let out a deep sigh. Uncle didn't seem to really be listening to them, so she didn't think she should bother until the Knight Protector returned. She took the scroll. It was identical to the one the bishop had shown her in the church.

"You kids should be with kin, not all locked up in some garrison somewhere." Uncle rested his axe on the ground, balanced by both hands holding the center of the bit. "That's what yer pa would want. Time's a-wasting; let's get on packing up."

HAVE YOU EVER FELT LED BY THE HOLY SPIRIT TO GO IN A
DIFFERENT DIRECTION THAN THOSE AROUND YOU?

PASSAGE QUESTIONS

Read the STORY PASSAGE and answer the following questions in your reading journal.

1. Whose return did the kids want to wait for?
2. Where did the person they were waiting on go?
3. Where does Uncle believe the kids should go?
4. Why does Uncle think that is the best place?

Joke of the Day

What did the sketchbook say to the novel?

I'm drawing a blank.

DAY FOUR

MEMORY VERSE, VOCABULARY & READING

In your reading journal, copy this week's memory verse and draw a picture definition for each vocabulary word. Then, read chapters seven and eight in the book.

STORY PASSAGE

Lauren continued, "Uncle said he's going to take us to grandma's house."

The elder warrior dropped the reins. "Your father's brother is here?" He scanned the yard. "Where is he?"

Aiden dashed over and scooped up the reins. "He's with Ethan at the creek right now, trying to catch Sparkle Frog."

Knight Protector put his hands on his hips and scanned the woods. "After our discussion this morning, do you think he's right to do this?"

Aiden was taken aback by this. He did agree that it seemed like the still small voice was telling them to go to Blooming Glen. Knight Protector was a stranger though, and Uncle was family.

"Well, he talked to Daddy and has his paper." The quiver in Aiden's voice gave away his uncertainty. "I don't know if he heard the small voice."

"I see." Knight Protector frowned. "And you, Lauren?"

"I believe Ethan's dream and your story about Daddy changing his mind. I'm worried about the consequences if we don't follow that."

WHAT CAN YOU DO IF YOU DISAGREE WITH THOSE IN CHARGE?

PASSAGE QUESTIONS

Read the STORY PASSAGE and answer the following questions in your reading journal.

1. Where do the children believe the still small voice is urging them to go?
2. Do the children believe Uncle heard the small voice?
3. Which sentence supports the previous answer?

Joke of the Day

Did you hear about the pen that can writer underwater?
It can write other words as well.

DAY FIVE

READING & MEMORY VERSE

Read chapter nine in the book. Then, recite this week's memory verse aloud and complete the activity below. Include the coloring page and vocabulary puzzle with today's activities.

ACTIVITY: AGED PAPER

MATERIALS

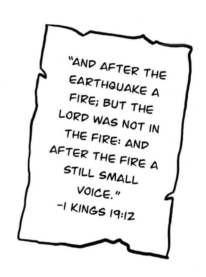

- A sheet of paper
- A ball-point pen or fine-point permanent
- Coffee
- Wax paper (or similar)
- Shallow container (large enough to submerge the sheet paper in coffee)

"AND AFTER THE EARTHQUAKE A FIRE; BUT THE LORD WAS NOT IN THE FIRE: AND AFTER THE FIRE A STILL SMALL VOICE."

–I KINGS 19:12

INSTRUCTIONS

Write this week's memory verse on a sheet of a paper (or another verse of your choosing). If desired, tear the edges of the paper for added effect. Place the paper in the container.

Next, brew a cup of coffee (cold leftover coffee also works) and fill the container with enough coffee to submerge paper. Let it sit for ten to twenty minutes (longer will produce a darker color).

Then, remove the paper and lay it on the wax paper overnight to dry.

WHY DOES SOAKING THE PAPER LONGER PRODUCE A DARKER COLOR?
HOW CAN WE APPLY THE SAME CONCEPT TO OUR WALK WITH GOD?

WEEK TWO
THE LOST

Memory Verse:
"*Now Samuel did not yet know the Lord, neither was the word of the Lord yet revealed unto him.*"
—1 Samuel 3:7 KJV

LAUREN

VOCABULARY

WORD LIST

As part of your daily work this week, you'll need to use a dictionary and a thesaurus to look up definitions, synonyms, and antonyms for the words below.

DRAMA   ORNATE   TALON
MALLET   POUNCE   UNISON

WORD SCRAMBLE

Rearrange each group of letters below to unscramble the words.

ATENOR

—— —— —— —— —— ——

ALETML

—— —— —— —— —— ——

ONUISN

—— —— —— —— —— ——

UNOPEC

—— —— —— —— —— ——

ALTNO

—— —— —— —— ——

ARADM

—— —— —— —— ——

DAY ONE

MEMORY VERSE, VOCABULARY & READING

In your reading journal, copy this week's memory verse and vocabulary definitions. Then, read chapters ten and eleven in the book.

STORY PASSAGE

Blood, water, what? Lauren felt he had completely lost it. She looked to the boys who shrugged. She did likewise. "Um… I guess that's right, but it's just gross."

Uncle did a double take. "Never mind that. What I'm saying is, family is the most important thing."

"Oh, I get it." Aiden raised his hand like he was in Sunday school. "Blood, like blood relations. But what's the water?"

"The water… it's a sayin': blood is thicker 'n' water." Uncle looked around the room for a minute like he was trying to find some example.

He shook his head. "We're kin, you see, and kin's got to stick together. So, you all need to stick with me, got it?" He put his hands on his hips. "I don't know what yer Knight Protector's plannin', but I do know yer gran would never forgive me if I let anything happen to you nibbles." He pointed at each of the children for emphasis, and then back at himself. "So, you need to follow my lead regardless of what kind of story the Knight Protector might be telling."

"OK, Coo Coo." Ethan looked at Aiden, then Lauren.

HOW CAN WE HANDLE DISAGREEMENTS IN A GODLY MANNER?

PASSAGE QUESTIONS

Read the STORY PASSAGE and answer the following questions in your reading journal.

1. What does Uncle mean by "blood is thicker 'n' water"?
2. How does Uncle feel about the Knight Protector's plan?
3. What evidence in the passage supports the previous answer?

> **Joke of the Day**
>
> Did you hear about the book on antigravity?
> It's impossible to put down.

DAY TWO

MEMORY VERSE, VOCABULARY & READING

In your reading journal, copy this week's memory verse and list three synonyms for each vocabulary word. Then, read chapters twelve and thirteen in the book.

STORY PASSAGE

The parson stepped to Ethan's side and slowly knelt on one knee. "Please, young Ethan, tell us about Sir Nicolas."

Ethan looked at the crowd and paused for a moment, not sure where to begin. Then he pointed toward their home. "Nicolas saved Sparkle Frog from the black water." Then he pointed at his siblings. "Then, he saved Sissy and Aiden from the bad dogs."

Ethan turned to Parson with a pleading look in his eyes. "He was my friend, and I miss him. Parson, please pray, and God will make him all better."

Parson's face fell at this request, leaving a lump in Ethan's stomach.

Ethan pleaded with his hands clasped together. "I prayed, and that wasn't good enough. You pray, and he will be all better."

"Oh child," the pastor pulled Ethan to him in a kind embrace. "I am so sorry. I know you and your brother and sister have prayed much over Nicolas." Ethan began to sob into Parson's shirt. The parson stroked Ethan's hair. "God has him home in heaven now to watch over us. His mission here on Earth is done, and he is now free of all the conflict and pain that still visits these lands."

WHAT DOES THE BIBLE SAY ABOUT HEAVEN?

PASSAGE QUESTIONS

Read the STORY PASSAGE and answer the following questions in your reading journal.

1. What happened to Sir Nicolas?
2. What did Ethan pray for?
3. What evidence in the passage supports the previous answer?
4. What did Parson say happened to Sir Nicolas?

Joke of the Day

Did you know I had plans to write a book about sinkholes?
Yeah, but they fell through.

DAY THREE

MEMORY VERSE, VOCABULARY & READING

In your reading journal, copy this week's memory verse and list three antonyms for each vocabulary word. Then, read chapters fourteen and fifteen in the book.

STORY PASSAGE

"Kids, we're leavin' for grandma's house. Now!" Uncle called over his shoulder.

Lauren's mouth dropped. She didn't even get a chance to make her case. *They were really going to grandma's house, even though the still small voice told them to go to Blooming Glen. How could she explain?*

"Uncle, wait," she said.

"Daylight's a burnin', little one. We need to get on down the road." The hard look on his face made it clear he wasn't going to listen.

This made her angry, and she was about to push the issue. Then, she realized that Uncle really didn't follow the Light, so anything she added right now would be met with skepticism. Grandma followed the Light though. Grandma was very wise, and she listened to the children. *Maybe Grandma can help us avoid the consequences.*

"Boys, I'm going to use my still small voice now." She hoped the boys would pick up on what she was trying to say. She climbed into the wagon and spoke to Aidan and Ethan quietly. "We need to go with Uncle to grandma's house. Grandma can help us with Mama and Daddy, I know it."

WHAT CAN YOU DO WHEN A SITUATION IS OUT OF YOUR CONTROL?

PASSAGE QUESTIONS

Read the STORY PASSAGE and answer the following questions in your reading journal.

1. Why was Lauren angry?
2. How did she deal with the situation that was making her angry?
3. Why does Lauren think there will be consequences?
4. How does Lauren hope to avoid the consequences?

Joke of the Day

My mom used to sprinkle my pillow with sugar.
She wanted me to have sweet dreams!

DAY FOUR

MEMORY VERSE, VOCABULARY & READING

In your reading journal, copy this week's memory verse and draw a picture definition for each vocabulary word. Then, read chapters sixteen and seventeen in the book.

STORY PASSAGE

Ethan watched as Aiden tied the falconer's cord to Daddy Duck's leg and his own wrist. As soon as he removed the hood, Daddy Duck took to the sky and jerked Aiden's arm up with him. Aiden wobbled like he was going to fall off the wagon, but then grabbed the wagon's side rail and steadied himself.

Ethan laughed at the wild display. After a couple of minutes of furiously trying to escape, Daddy Duck settled down and landed on the wagon seat. Then he let out an accusatory quack at Aiden, letting the boy know he was not happy with the current situation.

Before Aiden could respond, Daddy Duck noticed the worms on the seat. The frustrated duck let out another quack at Aiden and then picked up a worm in its bill and swallowed it. Then, the duck nestled down on the seat and gobbled up another worm, keeping an eye on Aiden.

"Hate to say I told you so, but a duck ain't no falcon," Uncle called up gruffly from where he had taken a knee to stoke the fire.

"He's just getting used to the idea."

HOW DOES UNBELIEF LIMIT US?

PASSAGE QUESTIONS

Read the STORY PASSAGE and answer the following questions in your reading journal.

1. What did Daddy Duck do when Aiden removed the hood from the duck's head?
2. What affect did his actions have on Aiden?
3. How did Ethan react to the situation?
4. Who said Daddy Duck was "getting used to the idea"?
5. Why did the person say that?

> **Joke of the Day**
>
> I fell asleep on a crossword the other day.
> I woke up with a puzzled look.

DAY FIVE

READING & MEMORY VERSE

Read chapter eighteen in the book. Then, recite this week's memory verse aloud and complete the activity below. Include the coloring page and vocabulary puzzle with today's activities.

ACTIVITY: INVISIBLE INK

MATERIALS

- Porous paper (like construction paper)
- Q-tip
- Lemon juice
- Small dish to hold the lemon juice
- Clothing iron

INSTRUCTIONS

Pour lemon juice into the small dish. Dip one end of the q-tip into the lemon juice and use it to write a message on the paper. Make sure the lemon juice saturates the paper well. Allow it to dry completely. Then, use a clothing iron set on high to apply heat to the paper on the side the message was written. Let the iron sit in place for about 30 seconds or so.

If you have any trouble revealing the message, check to make sure the lemon juice thoroughly saturated the paper and the heat was applied directly to the side on which the message was written. (Milk can be used as a substitute for lemon juice, but it doesn't work as well.)

HOW CAN WE REVEAL THE WORD OF THE LORD TO OTHERS?

WEEK THREE
IN THE BELLY

Memory Verse:
"Now the Lord had prepared a great fish to swallow up Jonah. And Jonah was in the belly of the fish three days and three nights."
—Jonah 1:17 KJV

ETHAN

VOCABULARY

WORD LIST

As part of your daily work this week, you'll need to use a dictionary and a thesaurus to look up definitions, synonyms, and antonyms for the words below.

BURR   HAUNCH   SPLAY
DIMINUTIVE   REFLEXIVE   TONIC

MAZE

Help the kids escape! Trace a path from the center of the maze to the outside.

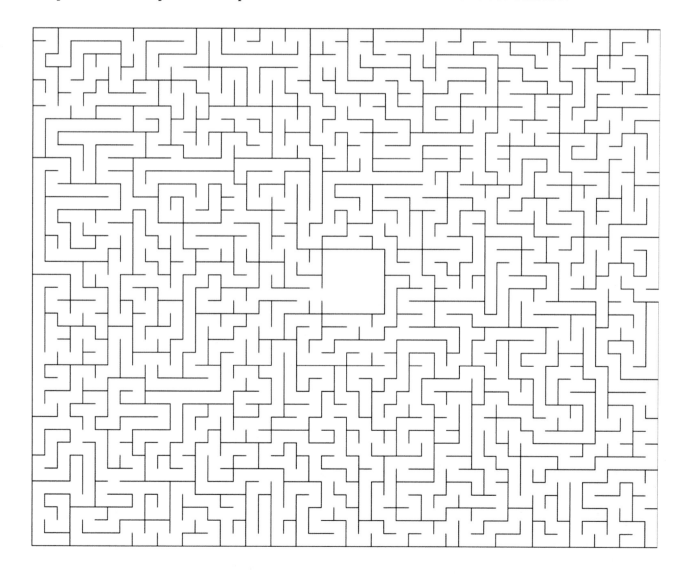

DAY ONE

MEMORY VERSE, VOCABULARY & READING

In your reading journal, copy this week's memory verse and vocabulary definitions. Then, read chapters ninteen and twenty in the book.

STORY PASSAGE

Lauren set her empty tin cup down and asked Ethan, "What are you thankful for?"

Ethan ran over and hugged Uncle. "I'm thankful for Uncle helping bring Sparkle Frog."

Uncle seemed to squirm under the hug, and his big eyes almost looked panicked by Ethan's sudden burst of emotion. He set down his cup and patted Ethan on the head. It surprised Lauren that Ethan was so affectionate after Uncle's treatment of Aiden the day before.

Aiden nodded his head. "I'm thankful Uncle helped bring Daddy Duck and that he teaches us stuff."

Lauren was not all that happy with Uncle's teaching methods. He could have helped Aiden with the duck the day before to keep him safe. She could feel heat in her cheeks, so she took a moment to compose herself. Then she picked up her kitten and petted him. "I'm thankful that Uncle let me bring Meow Meow."

Ethan let go of Uncle and stepped back, "What are you thankful for Uncle?"

Uncle raised his eyebrows and sat there slack jawed for a moment. "What? Why are you asking me?"

WHAT BLESSINGS ARE YOU THANKFUL FOR?

PASSAGE QUESTIONS

Read the STORY PASSAGE and answer the following questions in your reading journal.

1. How did Uncle feel about Ethan's words and embrace?
2. What evidence in the passage supports the previous answer?
3. Why was Lauren angry with Uncle?
4. Which sentence supports the previous answer?
5. What was Lauren thankful for?

Joke of the Day

My kids always have a tough time taking a nap, but I don't get it.
I can do it with my closed.

DAY TWO

MEMORY VERSE, VOCABULARY & READING

In your reading journal, copy this week's memory verse and list three synonyms for each vocabulary word. Then, read chapters twenty-one and twenty-two in the book.

STORY PASSAGE

Uncle stepped up to them and put the head of the double-bitted axe on the ground while he leaned on the handle. "Ain't no critter here in these parts that Ol' Faithful can't get the better of. Next time I tell you to go hide, I mean go hide. I can't fight well if I have to worry about you coming up to try to help. Got it?"

"Yes, sir," Lauren replied sheepishly, and the boys just nodded.

Uncle pointed at them. "Now put those things away and get back to bed."

"Yes, sir," they all responded despondently.

The boys put their arms away and followed Lauren down from the wagon, while Uncle walked to the fire. He added small branches to it and stoked it up considerably. Uncle dragged the cougar's carcass closer to the flames and began to skin it.

In the lean-to, Aiden whispered, "Sissy, why didn't you tell Uncle about the spear? It looked like you knocked the cougar out before he flipped it over and killed it."

"Yeah, Sissy? Why let Coo Coo take all the credit?" Ethan whispered.

How could she explain this to the boys? *God, you gave us these gifts, why don't people believe?*

HOW CAN WE DISCERN THE TRUTH?

PASSAGE QUESTIONS

Read the STORY PASSAGE and answer the following questions in your reading journal.

1. Why was Uncle upset?
2. What did Uncle want the children to do?
3. What happened to the cougar?
4. Why did the boys think Uncle shouldn't get all the credit for what happened to the cougar?
5. Why did Uncle not see Lauren's actions with the spear?

Joke of the Day

You know a few weeks back I spent all day writing a book about mazes. Yeah, I got lost in it.

DAY THREE

MEMORY VERSE, VOCABULARY & READING

In your reading journal, copy this week's memory verse and list three antonyms for each vocabulary word. Then, read chapters twenty-three and twenty-four in the book.

STORY PASSAGE

The daughter sat at a table with her mother's arm around her shoulder. "The night the censers exploded, there was chaos in the camp. I really don't remember how I got shuffled out of town—only that at one point, a giant threw me over his shoulder and carried me across a stream."

The matron's eyes flew wide as her mouth gaped open. "A Heath Warden, in league with the Darkness? If the giants have turned, these are truly dark days."

The acolyte was disturbed by this discussion. The censers brought the true light. With them destroyed, of course, bad things were bound to happen. He wanted to confront this heresy once and for all but decided it could wait for the rest of the story to be told.

He stood there for a moment, expecting her to continue. But the matron looked up. "Go on now, start getting ready for the lunch rush."

I need to know what happened.

The matron's upraised eyebrows and pursed lips showed him it was time to move along.

SHARE A TIME WHEN SOMETHING WAS NOT AS IT SEEMED.

PASSAGE QUESTIONS

Read the STORY PASSAGE and answer the following questions in your reading journal.

1. Who are the Heath Wardens?
2. Why is the acolyte disturbed by the discussion?
3. Does the acolyte follow the light or the darkness?
4. Was the acolyte eavesdropping?
5. Which sentence supports the previous answer?

Joke of the Day

Who was the greatest comedian in the Bible?
Samson. He brought the house down.

DAY FOUR

MEMORY VERSE, VOCABULARY & READING

In your reading journal, copy this week's memory verse and draw a picture definition for each vocabulary word. Then, read chapters twenty-five and twenty-six in the book.

STORY PASSAGE

Just then, a girl in a white robe like the boy servant came out of a side room. Her hair was wet and combed straight with a part down the middle, but she had scratches on her face and arms. *Oh, that looks owie. Maybe Sparkle Frog can help.* She scurried across the room and into the kitchen.

The matron turned back to Uncle. "My daughter will be speaking at church this evening and will tell you exactly what this has to do with ale."

Uncle investigated his empty mug. "I ain't exactly the goodness and light church type, ma'am."

"Maybe you should be," the matron retorted. "If more men sought the true Light, maybe this wouldn't have happened to my daughter."

Ethan hopped up and pulled on the matron's skirt. "She looks owie. Sparkle Frog makes head eggs go away." He patted the top of his head.

She looked down at Ethan with a broad smile on her face. "That's good to know, little one. But I'll take care of my own kin. Now you all eat your vittles, and when you're done, you'll get a bath and clean clothes."

TAKE A MOMENT TO PRAY FOR THE LOST.

PASSAGE QUESTIONS

Read the STORY PASSAGE and answer the following questions in your reading journal.

1. Why does Ethan think Sparkle Frog can help the girl?
2. Which sentence supports the previous answer?
3. What does the matron believe might have prevented the girl's attack?
4. Who is the matron referring to when she said "my own kin"?

Joke of the Day

How do we know Peter was a rich fisherman?
By his net income.

DAY FIVE

READING & MEMORY VERSE

Read chapter twenty-seven in the book. Then, recite this week's memory verse aloud and complete the activity below. Include the coloring page and vocabulary puzzle with today's activities.

ACTIVITY: BIRD FEEDER

MATERIALS

- Empty milk jug
- Stick or wood dowel, 8-12"
- String, 12-18"
- Birdseed, 2-3 cups
- Scissors
- Hot glue or outdoor Modge Podge
- Paints and markers, for decorating

INSTRUCTIONS

Wash and dry the empty milk jug. Use scissors to cut two openings on the sides opposite from the handle. The jug will need to hold birdseed in the bottom, so leave at least two inches from the edge on both sides of the opening and at least three inches from the bottom.

Poke two small holes near the lid on top and two slightly larger holes in the corner beneath the openings. Push the stick through the two holes near the bottom of the jug and hot glue it into place. (This will be a perch for the birds.) Next, thread the string through the two small holes on top—but don't tie it yet. This string will be used to hang the bird feeder. Once you've selected the right spot, you'll tie it then.

Decorate the outside of the jug as desired. After it dries, fill it with bird seed and hang it outside. (Tip: Mix red pepper flakes into the bird seed to deter squirrels. It doesn't bother birds. They can't taste it, but squirrels can.)

WEEK FOUR
HOLY SPIRIT

Memory Verse:
"Now we have received, not the spirit of the world, but the spirit which is of God; that we might know the things that are freely given to us of God."
1 Corinthians 2:12 KJV

VOCABULARY

WORD LIST

As part of your daily work this week, you'll need to use a dictionary and a thesaurus to look up definitions, synonyms, and antonyms for the words below.

BUGLE   HOLLER   TALL TALE
EPILOGUE   LEGEND   VERANDA

WORD SEARCH

Find and circle the hidden vocabulary words in the puzzle below. Words may appear up, down, forwards, backwards, or diagonally.

BUGLE	HAUNCH	ORNATE	SPLAY
BURR	HOLLER	PANTOMIME	TALL TALE
CRESCENDO	LACQUER	POUNCE	TALON
DRAMA	LEGEND	PROLOGUE	TONIC
DIMINUTIVE	MALLET	REFLEXIVE	UNISON
EPILOGUE	METAPHOR	SILHOUETTE	VERANDA

```
U N I S O N V S P L A Y R P R O L O G U E G I C Y
I S W D N L A C Q U E R F L K L F F H N Y I O W L
S T C T I B U G L E I T T P P Y E F D Q L A Z P C
G A H R C M V M A L L E T X L V T P Q R Z T Z D S
H L T G E R I Z L W R R M M H F B K I N A B L V K
R L G D K S E N G S I L H O U E T T E L U M U H I
Z T Z Y P L C F U E R O H O L L E R Y Y O Z A G X
H A T Z O M E E L T G M Z L D G X B U D H G G R Z
A L O J U E S G N E I P V R Z L Q G U O U H U R P
U E N C N T X B E D X V P A N T O M I M E N X E V
N I I R C A A U C N O I E I T V L I O R N A T E N
C I C Y E P C R M D D K V T H A G V E R A N D A E
H B E Z F H E R D J E Q T E Q K L Q X C F W Y A F
H E W A M O L A V C M I Q M Q W X O D I S F A K V
F Z I O Q R R P M M V X K P H A W L N N H N T V J
```

DAY ONE

MEMORY VERSE, VOCABULARY & READING

In your reading journal, copy this week's memory verse and vocabulary definitions. Then, read chapters twenty-eight and twenty-nine in the book.

STORY PASSAGE

"Save Bear!" Tok cried as he held his hand folded before him. "Pweeze"

"But Uncle said he didn't think we could do a scout without being seen." Aiden edged toward the hole in the barn.

"No, Uncle was worried about if we didn't have a guide we'd get caught." She pointed her spear at Tok. "We have a guide. I think he'll go on a scout with us."

Aiden shook his head. "Tok says the place is nearby. We can be sneaky. If it looks too dangerous, we can come get Uncle. If we ask for his help, he might just keep us locked up here, and poor Tok won't be able to get his bear."

"Yeah, Uncle never believes us, Sissy." Ethan jutted out his chin. "You beat that cougar, and he said he did."

Lauren slowly lowered her spear, shaking her head. "He told us he wouldn't even take us to spy things out. It feels dishonest to just go without telling him."

Tok's eyes filled with tears. *Would the girl not help now? She had to help!* "Save Bear?"

Ethan ran up and hugged Tok. This made him feel better, maybe the little one would help him.

HAVE YOU EVER BEEN ASKED TO HELP, BUT FELT YOU COULDN'T?

PASSAGE QUESTIONS

Read the STORY PASSAGE and answer the following questions in your reading journal.

1. Where are the kids?
2. Who asks the kids for help?
3. What does the person ask the kids to do?
4. Why are the kids uncertain about helping?
5. How does Tok react to the situation?

> ### Joke of the Day
>
> I'm not allowed to tell my teenager dad jokes anymore.
> He's laugh-toes intolerant.

DAY TWO

MEMORY VERSE, VOCABULARY & READING

In your reading journal, copy this week's memory verse and list three synonyms for each vocabulary word. Then, read chapters thirty and thirty-one in the book.

STORY PASSAGE

Ethan jumped up. "Yeah, like last night. Tok needed help, and we saved the Bear and broke the bad men's tent."

"You did what?" Uncle exclaimed, his eyes getting a wild look. Red rushed into his face.

No! Ethan, why'd you open your mouth? This is going to be a mess. Lauren attempted to diffuse the situation. "The creature we told you about was a Bjorn Born. The dark ones had captured his bear, and he needed help freeing it. Our weapons activated, so we knew we needed to help."

Uncle stood up, clenched his fists, and began to pace, looking at Lauren with clear anger in his eyes. "When I saw the mud on the hem of the boys' pants and a couple briars on yer skirt, I chalked it up to being in a dirty stable. But now you're telling me you left the stable and didn't tell me? What did I tell you kids about blood being thicker'n water?"

The hurt look on his face made the children feel ashamed of themselves. Uncle went over and picked up the Good Book.

"Yer pa was always Good Book this and that. It's clear that's all gone to yer heads."

WHAT ARE SOME COMMON MISCONCEPTIONS ABOUT THE BIBLE?

PASSAGE QUESTIONS

Read the STORY PASSAGE and answer the following questions in your reading journal.

1. Why did Uncle get angry?
2. How did Lauren feel about Ethan telling Uncle that they saved Bear?
3. What evidence in the passage supports the previous answer?

Joke of the Day

Why can't you tell your secrets to pigs?

They always squeal.

DAY THREE

MEMORY VERSE, VOCABULARY & READING

In your reading journal, copy this week's memory verse and list three antonyms for each vocabulary word. Then, read chapters thirty-two and thirty-three in the book.

STORY PASSAGE

"Uncle, we can beat him." Ethan branded his shield in the air.

Uncle paused. *Could they really do it?* Lauren's spear strikes had been dead on every time. Only the Light could give a little boy the power to cut clean through an axe.

Uncle looked back down the bridge; the giant had already cleared half of it. Now that he was closer, Uncle could see it was wearing some kind of harness and had some black iron contraption on his back that was spewing black smoke into the air. *I don't know what that is, but it can't be good.* He realized he was till holding the writ in an iron grip and shoved it into his waist pouch. Then tossed the torch where he thought it might best light the battle and pulled Ol' faithful off his back.

"Lauren, when he gets close enough, try yer spear." Uncle felt a tingle go up his spine and down his right arm. He looked at his hand and it seemed like Ol' Faithful had taken on the blue glow of Ethan's shield.

Must be seein' things, He shook his head and turned back to the advancing giant.

"Is that three little children playing warrior I see?" the giant bellowed as he strode across the bridge.

HOW DO WE BATTLE EVIL FORCES IN OUR WORLD?

PASSAGE QUESTIONS

Read the STORY PASSAGE and answer the following questions in your reading journal.

1. Who are Uncle and the children fighting?
2. What is spewing black smoke into the air?
3. Why does Uncle's axe seem to take on a blue glow like the children's weapons?

Joke of the Day

What do you get when you cross a pig with a centipede.
Bacon and legs.

DAY FOUR

MEMORY VERSE, VOCABULARY & READING

In your reading journal, copy this week's memory verse and draw a picture definition for each vocabulary word. Then, read chapters thirty-four and thirty-five in the book.

STORY PASSAGE

The geese landed gracefully in the dawn light. One on either side of the waterlogged figure floating on driftwood in the Awoi river. Their platinum feathers reflected the light all around them, making the area as bright as noonday. Each goose swam to a shoulder and ducked its head under an arm. They lifted their heads and pulled the big frontiersman up off the driftwood.

They floated with him down the river where it met the great Muddy River and on to Francis Ford. There they slowly waddled up onto the shore, with their charge in tow. Once he was out of the water, they put their heads down and walked back out from under his arms. Then, the geese patiently waited.

As the sun reached noon, the man's eyes opened. He slowly sat up on his elbows, and his eyes were dazzled by the glorious light reflected from the geese. A wave of peace and healing flowed over the man. "I'm still drawin' breath, so ain't no giant gonna hurt my nibbles."

HOW DOES SALVATION CHANGE US?

PASSAGE QUESTIONS

Read the STORY PASSAGE and answer the following questions in your reading journal.

1. Which river was the frontiersman floating on?
2. What time of day did he make it to shore?
3. How did he make it to shore?
4. When did the frontiersman finally open his eyes?

Joke of the Day

Why did the omelet flunk out of school?
　　It failed its eggs-zams.

DAY FIVE

READING & MEMORY VERSE

Read chapter thirty-six in the book. Then, recite this week's memory verse aloud and complete the activity below. Include the coloring page and vocabulary puzzle with today's activities.

ACTIVITY: 3D GLASSES

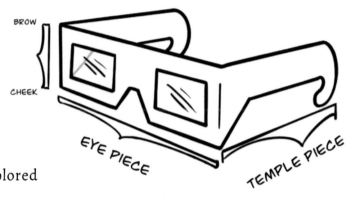

MATERIALS

- Glue or tape
- Ruler and scissors
- Red and blue markers
- Card stock or manilla folder
- Blue and red cellophane (clear, colored plastic binder dividers will work)

INSTRUCTIONS

First, measure from just behind your ear to you brow for the temple pieces. Then, measure across the face and from brow to cheek for the eye piece. Use these measurements to draw a template of your glasses onto a piece of card stock.

Next, cut out your glasses, including holes for the eyes. (Avoid cutting the glasses into multiple pieces. It works best if the glass frame is cut as one piece.) Decorate as desired.

The frame of your glasses can act as a guide to measure and cut out the lens. Cut at least one red and one blue lens from the clear, colored cellophane. (Adding a second or third layer of the cellophane to each lens can intensify the 3-D effect, so long as the layers aren't too thick to see through.) Glue or tape the lens into place.

Once your glasses are assembled, create a 3-D image by holding the red and blue markers together while drawing. Then, use your glasses to view it.

HOW DO WE DISCERN WHAT IS GOOD FROM WHAT ONLY LOOKS GOOD?

ANSWER KEY

WEEK ONE: A SMALL VOICE

DAY ONE

1. He means they are keeping information to themselves and not seeking advice from others.
2. "With the deception of the bishop and even my own behavior, it has to be difficult for you to trust anyone."
3. Ethan is more concerned about eating.
4. "He had a plate of bacon and flapjacks in front of him, and his stomach was aching."

DAY TWO

1. The Knight Protector discovered a Darkness machine.
2. Aiden was angry that the Knight Protector didn't knock it down.
3. "Aiden balled his fists and put them on his hips."
4. The Knight Protector didn't knock it down because the still small voice told him to wait and see.

DAY THREE

1. The kids wanted to wait for the Knight Protector.
2. The Knight Protector went to town to make plans to travel to Blooming Glen.
3. Uncle wants the kids to go to Gran's, their grandmother.
4. Uncle believes the kids should be with family and he has written instructions that specify the kids should go to Gran's.

DAY FOUR

1. The chldren believe the small voice is urging them to go to Blooming Glen with the Knight Protector.
2. No, they have doubts and are uncertain that Uncle has heard the small voice.
3. "The quiver in Aiden's voice gave away his uncertainty. 'I don't know if he heard the small voice.'"

SECRET MESSAGE

A crescendo of lacquer encased the silhouetted pantomine during the prologue as a silent metaphor.

WEEK TWO: THE LOST

DAY ONE

1. Uncle means that family loyalty is more important than loyalty to those who aren't family.
2. Uncle is suspicious and doesn't trust the Knight Protector.
3. Uncle tells the kids they need to stick with him and puts his hands on his hips. Then, he says, "So, you need to follow my lead regardless of what kind of story the Knight Protector might be telling."

DAY TWO

1. Sir Nicolas died.
2. Ethan prayed for Sir Nicolas to get better.
3. Ethan asked Parson to pray for Sir Nicolas to be all better. Then, Ethan said he prayed but it didn't work.
4. Parson said Sir Nicolas was in heaven, that his mission was complete, and he was free from pain and conflict

DAY THREE

1. Uncle wouldn't listen to her.
2. Lauren took a moment to realize that it wouldn't help to insist Uncle listen to her.
3. Because they aren't following the still small voice.
4. Lauren hopes her grandmother, who follows the Light, will help them.

DAY FOUR

1. Daddy Duck tried to fly away.
2. Aiden wobbled and had to grab the wagon's rail to keep from falling off.
3. Ethan laughed.
4. Aiden.
5. Aiden didn't want to admit defeat.

WORD SCRAMBLE

1. ATENOR: Ornate
2. ALETML: Mallet
3. ONUISN: Unison
4. UNOPEC: Pounce
5. ALTNO: Talon
6. ARADM: Drama

WEEK THREE: IN THE BELLY

DAY ONE

1. Uncle was embarrased, but pleased by the display of affection.
2. Uncle squirmed, looked panicked, and then patted Ethan on the head.
3. Lauren was angry about Uncle teaching methods.
4. "Lauren was not all that hppy with Uncle's teaching methods. He could have helped Aiden with the duck the day before to keep him safe."
5. Lauren was grateful Uncle let her bring her cat, Meow Meow.

DAY TWO

1. Uncle is angry the children joined the fight.
2. He wanted them to hide.
3. Uncle killed the cougar.
4. Lauren knocked it out first.
5. Uncle isn't a believer. He doesn't follow the Light.

DAY THREE

1. Heath Wardens are giants.
2. The acolyte believes the censors bring the one true light.
3. He follows the Darkness, but doesn't know it.
4. Yes.
5. The mother and daughter sat at table. The acolyte stood nearby and when the mother notices him, she tells him to start getting ready for the lunch rush.

DAY FOUR

1. Because Sparkle Frog healed him.
2. "Sparkle Frog makes head eggs go away."
3. She believes the girl's attack may have been prevented if more men sought the Light.
4. The matron is referring to the girl.

MAZE

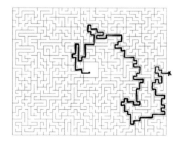

WEEK FOUR: HOLY SPIRIT

DAY ONE

1. They are in a barn.
2. Tok.
3. Tok asks the kids to help him save his bear.
4. The kids are uncertain about helping because their Uncle wouldn't even let them scout. He wanted the to stay where they were.
5. Tok's eyes fill with tears.

DAY TWO

1. The kids left the stable after he told them not to.
2. Worried.
3. Lauren thinks, *"No! Ethan, why'd you open your mouth?"* She also attempts to diffuse the situation.

DAY THREE

1. They are fighting a giant.
2. The iron contraption on the giant's back is spewing black smoke into the air.
3. Uncle is now a believer, and the Light is guiding him into battle.

DAY FOUR

1. The frontiersman was floating on the Awoi River.
2. It was around dawn when he was pulled ashore.
3. The geese carried him to shore.
4. It was around noon when he finally opened his eyes.

WORD SEARCH

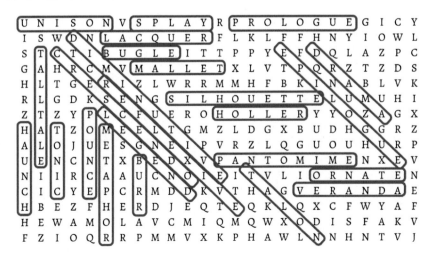

Made in the USA
Monee, IL
04 March 2023

28746991R00029